PAMPHLETS ON AMERICAN WRITERS · NUMBER 98

UNIVERSITY OF MINNESOTA

◢ *William Styron*

BY RICHARD PEARCE

UNIVERSITY OF MINNESOTA PRESS · MINNEAPOLIS

Printed in the United States of America at
the North Central Publishing Company, St. Paul

Library of Congress Catalog Card Number: 74-635458
ISBN 0-8166-0616-1

PUBLISHED IN THE UNITED KINGDOM AND INDIA BY THE OXFORD
UNIVERSITY PRESS, LONDON AND BOMBAY, AND IN CANADA BY THE
COPP CLARK PUBLISHING CO. LIMITED, TORONTO

FOR TUDY CAIRNS, WHOSE ASSISTANCE ON THIS PROJECT HAS
BEEN SO HELPFUL AND ENLIVENING

RICHARD PEARCE is an associate professor of English at Wheaton College in Massachusetts. He is the author of the book *Stages of the Clown: Perspectives on Modern Fiction from Dostoyevsky to Beckett* and has contributed to a number of literary journals.

⨯ William Styron

I‍N DISTINGUISHING the experience of his generation for *Esquire*, William Styron gives us a key to his fictional perspective and development:

In 1944, as a Marine recruit, I was shanghaied into the "clap shack," the venereal-disease ward of the Naval Hospital at Parris Island, South Carolina. There at the age of eighteen, only barely removed from virginhood, I was led to believe that blood tests revealed I had a probably fatal case of syphilis — in those pre-penicillin days as dread a disease as cancer — and was forced to languish, suicidal, for forty days and forty nights amid the charnel-house atmosphere of draining buboes, gonorrhea, prostate massages, daily short-arm inspections, locomotor ataxia, and the howls of poor sinners in the clutch of terminal paresis, until at last, with no more ceremony than if I were being turned out of a veterinary clinic, I was told I could go back to boot camp: I would not die after all, *it was all a mistake*, those blood tests had turned up a false reaction to an old case of trench mouth. I could have wept with relief and hatred. Such experiences have given our generation, I believe, both the means and the spirit to bridge the generation gap.

Having come of age during World War II, Styron saw his situation as radically different from that of the writers who influenced him most — Faulkner, Fitzgerald, Wolfe, and Hemingway. They were initiated by the Spanish Civil War, which, no matter how ferocious, was nevertheless remote. It left Americans disillusioned but intact. Styron's generation was not left intact. And its experience was not so much the failure or impotence of old values. For it was initiated by the atomic bomb and the senseless and overwhelming destruction of Hiroshima. It was "traumatized" by the war experience, by the "unimaginable presence" of the bomb, and by the feeling that the war was perpetual, was, in fact, the condition of life. World War II turned into the Cold War, whose "clammy presence oozed into our nights and days." And the Cold War turned into the Korean War, for which Styron, like so many of his contemporaries, was recalled to duty. The work which captures this situation most explicitly is *The Long March*, where the central characters, recovered from their experiences in Okinawa and fattened by the postwar prosperity, are recalled to train for the Korean battlefront, and Lieutenant Culver, the novella's narrator, realizes that "for six years they had slept a cataleptic sleep, dreaming blissfully of peace, awakened in horror to find that, after all, they were only marines, responding anew to the old commands." But the feeling of war as the condition of life pervades all of Styron's works: in *Lie Down in Darkness*, Peyton Loftis commits suicide on the day the bomb is dropped on Nagasaki; in *Set This House on Fire* Cass Kinsolving traces the beginning of his self-destructive striving to his experiences in World War II, which drove him to the psychiatric ward. And even *The Confessions of Nat Turner*, although set a full century earlier, is informed by the spirit of the battlefield.

Besides being inescapable, war is outrageously unreasonable. The enemy is undefined; heroic action becomes clownish and self-destructive. And Styron's early experience as a marine recruit "shanghaied into the 'clap shack'" is a paradigm. There is the ambush or senseless surprise, the absurd humiliation, and finally the realization that "it was all a mistake." What Styron shows in his most convincing fiction is, first, that beneath the calm and affluent exterior of modern life lies a violent potential, and, second, that this violence has a capricious life of its own and erupts as a senseless surprise, often in the form of an accident. He was feeling his way toward this vision in *Lie Down in Darkness* where, despite the influence of Faulkner, his characters are moved not by the logic of history but by ahistorical, irrational, and undefinable energies which burst through the mannered and manicured surface of their lives to drive them apart, frustrate connection, and deny psychological and aesthetic resolution. He realizes this vision most clearly in *The Long March*, by opening it with a senseless surprise: eight young marines are blown up in the misfiring of two mortar shells on a cloudless summer afternoon. In *Set This House on Fire*, Peter Leverett is initiated into the world of Sambuco by an accident with a crazy motorscooterist; and Cass Kinsolving is brought to his tragic awakening by a senseless surprise and a mistake: the accidental murder of Francesca by the hitherto harmless village idiot, and Cass's mistaken revenge and murder of Mason Flagg. The novel ends with Luciano having inexplicably recovered from his motorscooter accident and then, just as senselessly, falling down a flight of stairs to break his collarbone. And the senselessness of violence is even carried into the world of Nat Turner, when the revolutionary leader, in what could almost be seen as a cartoon caricature, bounces his mishandled ax or his dull sword off the heads of several victims, to have the job finished by the half-crazed Will, who emerges late in the novel, almost gratuitously.

Styron has not focused directly on the war experience which initiated him into manhood, but this experience informs all of his major fiction. Those who wrote of World War II saw it from one of two perspectives. James Jones, Norman Mailer, indeed most of the novelists who went through the war, viewed the battlefield from the prewar perspective. They still operated within naturalistic conventions and defined the social and psychological causes of their protagonists' condition. Joseph Heller, although he too fought in the war, viewed the battlefield from the postwar perspective and was quickly taken up by the new generation. He showed his world to be dominated by a runaway logic, and within his world there is no way to distinguish madness from sanity, reason from irrationality, selfishness from selflessness, nor is the mad destructiveness attributable to any social or psychological causes. Styron, in dramatizing war as the condition of life, developed a postwar perspective close to that of Heller and the next generation. Or perhaps it would be more accurate to turn his own phrase and see him as a "bridge" between two generations. With most writers of his generation he shares a faith in literature as a way to knowledge and order, and a faith in Christian humanism as a way to salvation. With the later generation he shares an apocalyptic, or neo-apocalyptic, view which denies the possibility of knowledge, order, or salvation.

The traditional apocalyptic view was dualistic or Manichean; it pictured a struggle between good and evil cosmic powers and revealed the present, irretrievably evil period of history headed for violent and complete destruction, to be followed by a new period, beyond history, of eternal harmony. The modern experience of apocalypse lacks a temporal or linear dimension. It is ahistorical and nonrational. It does not follow from anything, cannot be explained causally, cannot be justified morally, and does not look forward to a golden age of peace. It is an experience of violent and perpetual ending. Such an experience pervades the worlds of Peyton Loftis and Cass Kinsolving; both of these novels are charged with violent and irrational energies. *The Long March*, while far more tightly controlled, still reveals a world dominated by indefinable capricious forces; but, more importantly, it dramatizes the impotence of reason in explanation and moral guidance. The universe of the novel is dualistic, but there is no way of telling the forces of good from the forces of evil; and this is epitomized in the confrontation between Colonel Templeton, whose orders are both capriciously destructive and morally necessary, and Captain Mannix, whose rebellion is at once profoundly humanitarian and necessarily dehumanizing. The weaknesses in Styron's writing, especially in parts of his otherwise powerful *Set This House on Fire* and in the primary conception of *The Confessions of Nat Turner,* seem to arise when Styron substitutes a traditional, rational, and, in context, simplified apocalypse for the terrifying one he imaginatively discovered.

Styron also shares with the earlier generation a desire to see the world in heroic proportions; hence his use of myth in evoking the downfall of the Loftis family in *Lie Down in Darkness,* the crucifixion of Mannix in *The Long March,* the hubris of Cass in *Set This House on Fire,* the martyrdom of Nat Turner in *The Confessions.* But in each case the subject of his fiction is denied its heroic potential. *Lie Down in Darkness* remains a domestic tragedy, Mannix is turned into a clownish perpetrator of the very violence he rebels against, Cass is humiliated and must finally renounce his strivings. Except for *The Confessions of Nat Turner,* where I think Styron was working counter to his best imaginative instincts, the forces against which his characters contend cannot be confronted heroically. This is just their malicious quality. They end by reducing the protagonist, comically, by humiliating him. They are just like the forces that "shanghaied" young Styron into the "clap shack."

The senseless surprise, the absurd humiliation, and the final realization that it was all a mistake effect the ultimate violation in Styron's world. We should remember that violation is the end result of violence; it is an unjustified infringement, transgression, desecration, profanation, defilement, ravaging — primarily physical but finally psychological. The violation of Styron as a marine recruit was an exercise of violence as accident, of physical force inflicting profound psychological injury because it was undefinable in its source, immeasurable in its strength, unaccountable in its means of attack, unreasonable in its mistake. And Peyton Lof-

9

tis, Mannix, Cass, and perhaps even Nat Turner are all violated by such irrational powers.

The reaction to violence, unless one accepts it, is outrage. Outrage, Ihab Hassan reminds us, "implies excess, the passing beyond all bounds; it signals disorder, extravagance, fury, insolence; it refers to violent injury and gross and wanton offence. Outrage is rage without measure, but its secret rhythm is one of assault and protest, force and counterforce . . . an irrational dialectic of violence threatening the human form, the very nature of man. In this dialectic, action and reaction are compressed, beyond time, in a form of terrible unity." And according to Hassan, Styron's heroes follow in the tradition of Ivan Karamazov and Ahab, as "metaphysical rebels," struggling against a world which God created as "perpetually unjust," and perpetuating the unjust violence in the dialectic of their rebellions. Metaphysical rebels, yes, but not quite in the mold of Ivan or Ahab, for there is an unreasonable and indefinable force in the modern world which undermines their kind of heroic rebellion. William Faulkner recognized this, and the outrage that energizes his most powerful novels is in response to such a force. It was Faulkner whom William Styron chose as his first model.

Styron was born in 1925, in the shipbuilding center of Newport News, Virginia, and expected to find a career in engineering. Although two of his stories written before his first three-year tour of duty in the marines were published in a collection of creative writing at Duke University, it was only when he returned to Duke that he began to think about writing seriously. William Blackburn encouraged Styron to take Hiram Haydn's course on the novel at the New School of Social Research in New York City, and it was there that he conceived his first novel. Published in 1951, after three years' work (Styron has always been a slow writer),

Lie Down in Darkness was a remarkable achievement of imagination, observation, and control. A large cast of characters are, for the most part, fully imagined. The locale and manners of Tidewater society are sensitively observed and recorded. The novel, a collage of flashbacks from the day of Peyton Loftis' burial, is skillfully put together. And there is a rich range of style and pace in the narrative, the descriptions, and the dialogue, which includes a final tour de force in Peyton's interior monologue on the day of her suicide.

Lie Down in Darkness bears Faulkner's imprint, despite Styron's deliberate efforts to eliminate it. The structure, the key symbols, and many of the characters recall *The Sound and the Fury*, and the funeral procession seems to derive from *As I Lay Dying*. But Styron's novel takes on a life of its own, and its success, indeed a major element of the fictional experience, depends on Styron's movement away from Faulkner and the world view of the twenties. Faulkner was outraged at what had become of a tradition grounded in aristocratic and Protestant values, values which he was to discover were simultaneously and unreasonably humane and life-denying. And his outrage was focused on history, or the passing of time. In *Lie Down in Darkness*, despite the literary allusions, there is almost no sense of passing time, no real connection between the present and a past that contained its communal and sustaining values. And despite the preponderance of flashbacks the novel is all present. Unlike Faulkner, who shows us a present rising out of an ambiguous past, Styron shows us a past that is part of the ambiguous present.

"At precisely eleven o'clock on a weekday morning in August of 1945, a black, shiny hearse, whose motor was so soundless that the effect was that of no motor at all, slid to a stop on the station dock at Port Warwick." But the motor turns out to be not so soundless after all, for while there are innumerable narrative lines leading back to important moments in the lives of all the major characters, the hearse carrying Peyton's body to the cemetery will remain central: it will serve, in its realistic detail and comic irrelevancy, to ground remembrance and rhetoric in the chaotic and sweltering reality of the present moment. For instance, Milton Loftis is waiting in a limousine behind the hearse for the arrival of his daughter's body. He carries us back in time by recollecting his father, who, with echoes of Mr. Compson, admonishes, *"I do not propose to convince you merely through paternal advice which no doubt you in your willful notion of filial duty would abjure anyway. . . ."* And this rhetorical flight from the present leads us through Milton's university days, when at the age of nineteen he was "a sot even by fraternity standards," and through his career in the army to his enviable marriage with the colonel's daughter. We are then drawn back to the present by a boat whistle to see Loftis still in his reveries, looking "up through the dust, the slanting frames of light," and reaching for the hand of his wife, Helen, who is not there, and now trying to escape once more. " 'No!' he cried. 'I can't go through with it!' " But the reader is forced to go through with it, for he cannot escape. We are brought back to the insistent necessity of the present. "The hearse was parked near the coal elevator. Each time Mr. Casper bent over to explain to Barclay what was wrong with the motor, a gondola car was upturned on the tracks above them, and his words were lost in the furious roar of coal." And what follows is a realistic description of men repairing the hearse's radiator — realistic in its careful recounting of detail and in its comic irrelevancy to Loftis' preoccupations.

If the hearse continually brings us back to the present moment in time, it also brings us back to the present position in space. After a long flashback, which takes us through the suburbs where Helen discovers Milton's infidelity, confronts Dolly Bonner in a tea shop, and turns for relief to the Reverend Carey Carr, we see the hearse stalled in a long line of cars behind the stoplight at Thirty-Fourth and Virginia: "Barclay ground away on the starter, but the hearse didn't move, and from all sides came the noise of car horns, irreverent and frantic in the noonday heat." The hearse serves to stall us, to fix us, in the mundane present. And if, with its implacable reminder of Peyton's death, it begins to suggest a meaningful connection between past events and the present moment, the connections are never made for us in the fabric of the novel and are in fact undermined by the continual insistence of physical irrelevancy. There is no connection between the places where the hearse — accidentally — stops and any places in the lives of the main characters. Nor is there any connection between the physical details so sharply reported in these scenes and any details in the main story line — and the contrast is enforced by the contrast in tone, pace, and diction. The continual insistence of irrelevancy in the present makes flight into the past — for either escape or meaning — futile. While Faulkner fractured his narrative and the objective continuum of time in *The Sound and the Fury* to discover meanings in the subjective time patterns of his characters, Styron fractures his narrative to destroy whatever connections of causality and meaning might be gained by his flights into the past.

It is at just this point that Styron begins to work away from Faulkner and the earlier generation of writers. Not completely, for there is still much in his perceptions and his style that ties him to them, especially to F. Scott Fitzgerald. Hence, Peyton laments to Dick Cartwright, "Those people back in the Lost Generation. Daddy, I guess. Anybody who thought about anything at all. They thought they were lost. They were crazy. They weren't lost. What they were doing was losing us." Daddy, in fact, did not think of anything, at least not in the way Peyton suggests. He drifted helplessly through life — through the university, where he became a sot, into marriage with the socially attractive Helen, through professional failures, and into an alliance with Dolly. If he thought of anything it was only of Peyton, to whom he was incestuously attracted. And the reader, like Peyton, is led to search for links between his incestuous desires, his drinking, his failures, his infidelity, Helen's neurotic connection with her crippled daughter, Maudie, her hatred of Peyton, of men, and even of women as sexual vessels.

One weakness of the novel may be attributed to Styron's ambivalence. Part of his mind was conditioned by the ideas and the sensibility of those writers who most influenced him. But, as his next two novels clearly show, he was working imaginatively away from such influences. If the novel's weakness is due to his ambivalence, its strength lies in its movement from the world of the twenties to the world of the fifties, in its independence, and even, considering when it was written, its prophetic qualities.

In 1954, three years after publishing *Lie Down in Darkness*, and having received the Prix de Rome, he was interviewed for the *Paris Review*. Perhaps feeling his oats, he told the interviewers that having Peyton commit suicide on the day the atomic bomb was dropped was "just gilding the lily. If I were writing the same thing now I'd leave that out and have her jump on the Fourth of July." But sixteen years later he insisted that his generation had been initiated by the atomic bomb and the destruction of Hiroshima, and the never-ending sense of impending or potential warfare. Moreover, the war and the bomb are not imposed on the experience of *Lie Down in Darkness*; we are made to feel the impending threat of irrational destruction beneath the polished surface of the suburban world and in the very texture of the novel.

When war is the condition of life, the experience is open ended, open at both ends. And this experience, epitomized in the explosion of the first atomic bomb, was quantitatively and qualitatively different from that of Styron's predecessors. In 1945 a quantum gap was opening, and Styron was among the first writers to respond to it imaginatively. The war which began as a "hard-boiled matter of stamping out a lot of very real and nasty totalitarianism" ended on a note of violent irrationality, which was fully realized some years later by many who experienced the Cold War and the Korean War. It was at that point when what is now called the post-modern sensibility was being shaped, out of a feeling that the old rational laws of cause and effect made little sense.

Lie Down in Darkness is structured to undermine causal connections between past, present, and future. Although Styron is often at his best, in all of his novels, when developing an engaging plot line, he was working toward what Earl Rovit, in reference to another group of writers, has described as an "apocalyptic structure" — which has no center, no organic connections, only energy and fragments of an exploding surface. With no causal connections, no organic nexus, there are no physical, emotional, psychological, or ethical directions. The biblical experience of apocalypse was eschatological; it derived from a sense of the final struggle between warring powers of good and evil. But the modern experience of apocalypse goes beyond this and expresses a total nihilism and chaos; there is neither a sense of ending nor a sense of beginning, nor can the warring powers be ethically designated.

The central struggle, or agon, in *Lie Down in Darkness* is between Peyton's father and her mother. But how are we to describe the agon? Not in terms of good and evil or right and wrong. We cannot describe it at all, because the source and even the field of the agon is out of sight. There are only a few memorable clashes — one when Dolly begins her flirtation with Milton and

Peyton ties up Maudie, one at Peyton's birthday party, and one at her wedding. Rather, the agon between Milton and Helen is dramatized with great skill in their centrifugal reactions to one another, in the energy, that is, which drives them apart. This is primarily accomplished through the shifting points of view which focus now on Milton and his relation to Dolly, now on Helen and her relation to Carey Carr. All the while we sense that Milton is drawn toward Dolly, and Helen toward Carr, by forces which are driving Milton and Helen apart. But we never see the source of this energy, and we never see the agon itself. We only see the symptoms or the effects in Milton's drinking, drifting, sentimentality, and incestuous desires; in Helen's morbid love for the crippled Maudie, her neurotic revulsion from sex, her developing religiosity.

Peyton's story is not one of the loss of innocence, as so many critics conclude. There is nothing for her to lose. She is desperately striving for an emotional, psychological, and ethical center. On the day of her wedding to Harry she tries to make her father understand this. "Don't you see, don't you see, Bunny? I come back here all sweetness and light trying my best to play the good sweet role, the prodigal daughter. . . . I've got my own reasons for coming home. I've wanted to be normal . . . to be able to say, 'Well now my rebellion's over, home is where I want to be.'" Rebellion is the wrong word, although it is the only word in Peyton's vocabulary that can express the feel of her drive and movement. But rebellion must be against something, must have some fixed source. And in her world, torn by the forces driving her mother and father, there is no center that Peyton can reach toward or run away from. New York is not a rejection of her home; the novel opens and closes with the train which joins New York and Port Warwick, making them part of the same fabric. Harry is no rejection of Milton; he is, rather, a substitute which must also be rejected. And the crude and brutal Tony is no rejection of Harry, for he serves the same ambivalent need, which is to strike outward and inward at the same time.

The powerful interior monologue which concludes the story of Peyton Loftis works in a way that is diametrically opposed to its prototype in *Ulysses,* and serves to distinguish Styron's and Joyce's worlds. It does not give us a sense of formal or psychological unity, but is fully expressive of Peyton's apocalyptic experience. While Molly Bloom is almost continuously inert, Peyton is continually in motion. The frantic emotional and physical pace of this section contrasts dramatically with that of all the other narrative lines in the novel, especially the one carrying the hearse to the cemetery. Peyton is driven from Tony's to the bar to Lennie's to Berger's to Harry's, and finally to Harlem, where she jumps out of a bathroom window; the violence of her energy is reinforced by the repeated references to the atomic bombs which have just been dropped on Hiroshima and Nagasaki. And her irrational physical movement is complicated by her stream of consciousness, which is not really a stream, for the recollections do not seem to flow from one association to the next; they seem to explode out of her wild unconscious — disconnected moments of the past driven irrationally into the present. The violent energy is also expressed in the images that surface, especially the flying birds and the sense of drowning. The birds symbolize innocence, purity, freedom, and also the avenging furies of her conscious and unconscious guilt. Drowning is a symbol of orgiastic forgetfulness and of renewal. But, more important, together the images of flying and drowning evoke the contradictory and centrifugal movement that dominates the novel, the force that drives Milton and Helen apart and denies Peyton a stable center of emotional and moral reference.

Peyton's suicide ends with a note of resurrection: "Myself all shattered, this lovely shell? Perhaps I shall rise at another time, though I lie down in darkness and have my light in ashes." This is not in character for Peyton, despite the religious influence of her mother. And Styron must have sensed this, for he ends the novel with an entirely different kind of religious experience. At the Negro baptism, entirely irrelevant to the story line, the crowd looks out at the raft to see embroidered on the damask curtain "dragons and crosses and crowns, Masonic emblems, shields, bizarre and unheard-of animals . . . all these glowed against the curtain in green and red phosphorescent fabrics, literally hurting the eyes." Finally the majordomo appears, "Gabriel, chief lieutenant: a personage with a stern, muscular face . . . without modesty, almost contemptuously." When he speaks of the King of Glory, he stands "stern and erect and unperturbed, his robe a blue splash against the red shields and green prophetic talismans and crawling dragons." And he is followed by a shriek "like the first firecracker on a string, and it set off an explosion of yells."

This scene has an immediacy only matched by that of Peyton's monologue and the realistic descriptions of the hearse — three facets of the immediate present. The hearse serves to bring us back from the past to the present, to make the past part of the present in a volatile and unintelligible pattern. The baptism scene is also part of this present, and is grounded in realistic asides. "La Ruth belched. 'Stonewall,' she said, 'come on in here outa dat water! Put on dem sandals, boy. You gonna snag yo' feet on a oyshter.' " The experience of the baptism recalls the Book of Revelation, and the militant Gabriel connects it with the experience of irrational warfare that boils just beneath the surface of the novel. When Daddy Faith finally appears to the sound of a trumpet, he is a ridiculous figure, "a round tub of a man, as black as black ever could get. . . . He stood at the edge of the raft, smiling, benign, avuncular." And beneath the lamp which flickered LOVE, he announces that "de people of Isr'el done gone off to war . . . and dey sent down de atom bomb on de Land of de Risin' Sun and de sojers come home wid glory in dey th'oats and wid timbrels and de clashin' of bells." The realistic detail and the comic irrelevancy of this scene make it a parody of the religious resolution of *The Sound and the Fury.* The baptism does not wash away the sins of the world, as Ella Swan believes, nor does the religious experience offer any hope of resurrection or even of endurance. Instead it exposes the reality existing beneath the polished suburban surfaces and southern manners, and gives ultimate expression to the forces tearing apart the world of Peyton Loftis.

In his neglected novella, *The Long March,* first published in 1953 in *discovery No. 1,* Styron sacrificed range to find a form which expressed the human situation with conciseness and clarity, and in which he could affirm the values of Christian humanism in a way that was consistent with his vision.

At one point the protagonist describes the most frightening experience in his life:

"We were drunk, you see, polluted, all of us. I think there were five of us, all of us boots just out of Dago. Kids. We were on the tenth floor of this hotel and in this room and I believe we were about as drunk as anyone could get. I remember going in to take a shower in the bathroom. It was late at night, past midnight, and after I took this shower, you see, I came out into the room buck naked. Two of those drunk guys were waiting for me. They grabbed me and pushed me toward the window. I was so loaded I couldn't battle. Then they pushed me out the window and held me by the heels while I dangled upside-down buck naked in space, ten floors above the street." He paused and sucked at a beer can. "Can you imagine that?" he went on slowly. "How I felt? I got stone-sober in a second. Imagine being that high upside-down in space with two drunks holding onto your heels. I was heavy, man, just like now, you see. All I can remember is those teeny-weeny lights below and the tiny little people like ants down there and those two crazy drunk guys holding onto my wet slippery ankles, laughing like hell and trying to decide whether to let go or not. I just remember the cold wind blowing on my body and that dark, man, infinite darkness all around me, and my ankles beginning to slip out of their hands. I really saw Death then, and I think that all I could think of was that I was going to fall and smash myself on that hard, hard street below. That those crazy bastards were going to let me fall. I was praying, I guess. I remember the blood rushing to my brain and my ankles slipping, and that awful strange noise. And I was reaching out, man, clutching at thin air. Then I wondered what that noise was, that high loud noise, and then I realized it was me, screaming at the top of my voice, all over San Francisco."

Here Styron found a metaphor of the human situation toward which he had been reaching in *Lie Down in Darkness*, which he was to express more diffusely in *Set This House on Fire*, and which would even inform *The Confessions of Nat Turner*; it recalls his experience as a marine recruit "shanghaied into the 'clap shack.' " In an environment that is urban, military, and dark, man is surprised, ambushed, senselessly assaulted — not to the end of defeat or destruction, not to any end at all. He is suddenly and capriciously turned upside down, turned from a man with potentials of dignity and heroism into a helpless clown acutely aware of life's terror. This terror is caused not by a hostile power or even by an indifferent universe, but by a wanton sporting with individual life — "Imagine being that high upside-down in space with two drunks holding onto your heels."

The Long March is similar in many ways to Melville's *Billy Budd*. In both works the thematic conflict is between the innocent individual and the representative of social necessity. In both works social law is made manifest in a military order. In both works the hero's instinctive reaction to human injustice has immediate destructive consequences for his associates and for himself. Both works end in a martyrdom that is in fact socially just. But the difference between *The Long March* and *Billy Budd* is signal; the view of life after World War II is sharply differentiated from that of earlier periods. Melville dramatizes the tragic price of human preservation and social harmony; Captain Vere, as he condemns Billy, is deeply aware of this price. Colonel Templeton knows that military order and soldierly discipline are necessary on the battlefield, but despite his sensitivity, integrity, and realistic logic, the end he serves is not a human harmony, as it was with Vere. In fact the end is obscured from the sightlines of the novella.

The kind of war depicted in *The Long March* is just the kind of purposeless and pervasive war we have come to know so well in the second half of the twentieth century. For this is not World War II, the justice of which could guarantee some meaning to death and destruction. It is not even the battleground of the Korean War, where, despite the senselessness, there was still an identifiable enemy. This is a marine training maneuver. The enemy "was labeled Aggressor, on maps brightly spattered with arrows and symbolic tanks and guns, but although there was no sign of his aggression he fled them nonetheless and they pushed the sinister chase, sending up shells and flares as they went."

Captain Mannix, a Brooklyn Jew, and Lieutenant Culver, from whose viewpoint the story is told, are veterans of World War II who, having adjusted to the postwar prosperity, and being now too old and flabby for effective service, have been called back to train for the Korean War by the unreasonable and impractical mechanism of the reserve system. The book opens with an accident. Two mortar shells have misfired and exploded among a group of lunching recruits: "One noon, in the blaze of a cloudless Carolina summer, what was left of eight dead boys lay strewn about the landscape, among the poison ivy and the pine needles and loblolly saplings." In the first sentence Styron pictures the irrational violence exploding from beneath the placid surface of life, expressing explicitly and with sharper clarity a view that he had begun to conceive in his story of Peyton Loftis, and which would dominate the world of Cass Kinsolving.

Styron drew on his own experiences in 1950, when he was recalled to marine duty during the Korean War and compelled to participate in a forced training march. Within a realistic framework he develops the contradictory irrational potential — the destructive irrationality and an irrational affirmation — with the aid of comic devices. The central conflict is caused not by a direct and clearly embodied hostility, as it is in *Billy Budd*, but by Colonel Templeton's impersonal and apparently irrational order for a thirty-six-mile forced march. Mannix's determination to assert the human value of his own person and of his men in the featureless face of the Marine Corps is also irrational; and Lieutenant Culver finds himself in a situation similar to Peyton's, caught between warring powers which cannot be ethically distinguished. Captain Mannix tries to achieve his end in an action that is doubly irrational: he will defy the colonel by driving his men to achieve the impossible, which is to complete the march. And his defeat is accomplished far less in the prospective court-martial than it is in the picture of the heroic captain turned into a clown, gratuitously wounded by a nail in his shoe, "toiling down the road with hobbled leg and furious flailing arms." And even more by the irony of his being turned into Templeton's accomplice: "You're goddam right, Jack. . . . My company's going to make it if I have to *drag in their bodies.*"

The world is surely upside down when we see Mannix, with his compassion and sense of justice, fulfilling the role of Satan and Templeton assuming the role of priest. This in indeed the kind of hell Mannix saw as he dangled high up in space with two drunks holding onto his slippery heels. And in the confrontation between Mannix and Templeton Styron creates a modern version — or inversion — of the confrontation in Dostoevski's "Grand Inquisitor."

Still, we come to realize that this has all been a preparation for a final inversion. *The Long March* ends with a comic recognition. Back in their quarters Mannix, coming out of the showers, encounters the Negro maid, who looks at him and says, "Oh my, you poor man. What you been doin'? Do it hurt? . . . Oh, I bet it does. Deed it does." Mannix looks at her silently, blinking, as she repeats, "Deed it does." And "almost at precisely the same instant, the towel slipped away slowly from Mannix's waist and fell with a soft plop to the floor; Mannix then, standing there, weaving dizzily and clutching for support at the wall, a mass of scars and naked as the day he emerged from his mother's womb, save for the soap which he held feebly in one hand. He seemed to have neither the strength nor the ability to lean down and retrieve the towel and so he merely stood there huge and naked in the slanting dusty light and blinked and sent toward the woman, finally, a sour, apologetic smile, his words uttered, it seemed to Culver, not with self-pity but only with the tone of a man who, having endured and lasted, was too weary to tell her anything but what was true. 'Deed it does,' he said."

As the story progressed Mannix had become more and more ridiculous, and more destructive and fanatic than even Colonel Templeton. But with the shift in tone, tempo, and perspective in the final scene, he is reestablished as humane and heroic. We end the book with contradictory views of Mannix, and with the non-rational experience of having come to a deep understanding of the very values which were abrogated by Templeton and the facts of reality. Styron achieved this effect by a double inversion. First

23

he turned the world upside down to convey the full terror of a world governed by capricious forces, and to show man senselessly surprised, ambushed, reduced, and humiliated. Here Styron was following in the long tradition, revived in the 1950's, of writers who evoked the incongruous terror and the gratuitous surprises of an absurd universe through comic means. Then, again, he turned the world upside down to illuminate old values in a new light. Here the comedy works to surprise us, through inversions of accepted views, into a fresh awareness: "Christ on a crutch" turns out to be a kind of Christ after all.

In *The Long March* Styron was able to clarify his vision and develop its ironies through an effort of concentration. Now he needed to expand, to find a form with space and scope commensurate with his vision's range and intensity. The background of *Set This House on Fire* (1960) resembles the civilian world out of which Mannix and Culver were called. There is the middle-class world of Peter Leverett, who functions as a kind of Nick Carraway, sensitive, innocent, firmly rooted in the social system and drawn first to the demonic Mason Flagg and then to the rebellious Cass Kinsolving. There is also the lower-class world of Cass, whose experience of the South was remote from Peter's. And there is the upper-class world of Mason Flagg — the splendid estate where he tells "Wendy-dear," his mother, that he was expelled from prep school again, this time for being caught in the chapel basement "stark naked with the weak-minded daughter of a local oysterman, both of them clutching bottles of sacramental wine." But in the foreground of the novel is Sambuco, Italy, inhabited by an American movie company, Mason Flagg, who is ostensibly writing a novel, and Cass Kinsolving, who, at the end of a long European debauch, is ostensibly trying to paint.

Italy was a good choice for the central action. It has traditionally been a kind of Arcadia for American writers and artists and functions ironically in the pattern of Cass's development. It was a major battleground for World War II and one seat of totalitarianism, and the experiences of war and totalitarianism are seminal in the novel. It was becoming a caricature of America and allowed Styron to gain some distance on his main subject.

Sambuco is situated high up on a mountain, overlooking a "magnificent sea" and a "barbaric valley" and slopes upon which "some wretched poor sheep were grazing." When Leverett arrives at the gothic piazza, he finds himself "exposed to a battery of cameras and arc lights and reflectors, and now to the pop-eyed rage of a roly-poly little man in Bermuda shorts bearing down upon me, his lips curled around the butt of a cigar." The aggressive incongruity between the movie set with its glitter of American affluence and the stark Italian countryside with its implacable poverty recalls an incongruity of American life to which we are only now beginning to give full recognition. Leverett's father, a southern liberal, sees his fellow Americans as a "bunch of smug contented hogs rooting at the trough. Ciphers without mind or soul or heart. Soap peddlers!" And he tells his son that "what this great land of ours needs is something to happen to it. Something ferocious and tragic, like what happened to Jericho." This is the experience — the setting of his house on fire — that Leverett goes through vicariously as he listens to the story of Cass Kinsolving.

The novel continuously penetrates the meretricious physical, social, and psychological façade of American life. Moreover, it dramatically contrasts the façade with the senselessly violent irrationality it covers. The form of the novel has two major elements. First there is the narrative dialogue between Peter and Cass at Cass's home in South Carolina two years after the main action; this element is dominated by Peter's quest for knowledge. The second element is the plot, which is the subject of Peter and Cass's dialogue, and which is dominated by Cass's quest for salvation. Peter knew Mason Flagg long before Cass met him, they were at prep school together; but all he knew of Cass was that he was a masochistic alcoholic playing the obscene buffoon to Mason at Sambuco. And all he knew of the main story was that Mason raped the beautiful Francesca and possibly killed her, and that Mason himself was dead. He feels in some way responsible for Mason's death, and, as Cass reveals the true story, he undergoes a vicarious purgation.

A weakness of *Set This House on Fire* may derive from Styron's faith in the traditional forms of novel writing and in the redemptive possibilities of Christianity. Both the narrative dialogue and the plot are strongly linear, and in both there is a promise of fulfillment. But the powerful experience Styron evokes is not linear; it denies the possibility of epistemological, theological, and psychological progress. The total effect of the novel, however, accommodates its weakness, and reinforces its main theme, which is the contrast between meretricious and worn-out forms and the irrational and destructive energies which will not be contained by them.

This contrast is also dramatized in a dialectic of styles. Robert Gorham Davis, the most sensitive critic of Styron's style, criticizes the "worked-up unbelievable quality" of the action, and compares the "day dream quality" of Cass's romance with Francesca with that of Mason's wartime romance — which, like Gatsby's tale of Oxford, he fabricates. Davis sees Mason's fabrication as a model for the novel, which is a rich and elaborate fiction referring to nothing at all. Still, he honestly confesses to being dissatisfied with his evaluation, for there is too much life in the novel. What Davis fails to recognize is that the surface, worked-up, daydream quality — especially as it contrasts with the violent current of Cass's action and the turbulent undercurrent of his nightmares —

creates the texture and meaning of the novel. The action of the novel does not work like Hemingway's, as an "objective correlative" to the protagonist's emotions. Like Peyton's monologue, it is driven by unfathomable energies expanding in all directions at once and exploding fragments from the surface. It conveys the nightmare world of which Cass, in his rebellion against it, is a manifest part.

Peter Leverett's Italian experience begins with a senseless surprise, ambush, and accident. Driving through the suburbs of Naples, he hears a noise from behind, "abrupt and thunderous, a shocking din which partook both of a salvo of rockets and an airplane in take-off." He escapes a rear-end collision, the driver passing him perilously "with a noise like a string of firecrackers, and with the central finger of one fist raised in ripe phallic tribute." Peter chases him unsuccessfully; then, falling "into aching oppressive woolgathering," he smashes broadside into a motorscooter. The driver, Luciano di Lieto, has a history of accidents: he cut off two fingers at the age of twelve poking around in an automobile engine; he broke both legs and permanently injured an elbow when he wandered in front of a Neapolitan streetcar; and, "only months after this, barely out of his casts, experimenting with fireworks at a seaside *festa*, he bent his dark, crazy regard down upon the muzzle of a Roman candle, and blew out his right eye." At the very end of the novel, Leverett, having assuaged his guilt like a good American by paying the monthly hospital bills, learns that Luciano has recovered, has risen, ostensibly like Cass, from his own ashes. But he also learns that right after his release from the hospital Luciano suffered another accident by falling down a flight of stairs and broke his collarbone. The nurse writes Leverett in lines that close the novel, "The durability of this young man is truly remarkable! I have just now come from seeing him, where he is sitting up in bed, cheerfully smiling and eating like a pig. He sends his felicitations to you, and tells me that he has become affianced. I do somewhat pity the girl but I do not doubt that, if she is at all like Luciano, it will be a match of long duration. He will live to bury us all."

The Luciano story is a comic frame for the serious plot of the main story; regeneration, as in traditional comedy, is expressed in a marriage which parallels the blissful reconciliation of Cass to his family. But the comic Luciano has a tragic double, the idiot Saverio, whose murder of Francesca is another surprise, ambush, and accident. And we recall that in our last view of Saverio "he was babbling happily and didn't seem to have any knowledge or recollection of what he had done." Moreover, the picture of Luciano "cheerfully smiling and eating like a pig" reminds us of the caricature of Americans given by Peter's father — "a bunch of smug contented hogs rooting at the trough." Luciano is a comic reminder of the wanton and gratuitous power that Americans in their affluent contentment refuse to recognize. We are led to feel that the condition of life evoked seriously in the Cass-Mason line and comically in the Leverett-Luciano line will continue. And perhaps that Cass, rather than finding himself as an artist and as a man, merely finds a way to escape the reality of modern life as he draws cartoons, teaches amateurs, and fishes in the idyllic backwaters of South Carolina.

The implacable dark and turbulent undercurrent, which will not accommodate itself to either the redemptive promises of Christianity or the formal container of the traditional novel, is evoked in the excesses of style, which express the disproportion between dramatic activity and suppressed reality, in the long and powerful descriptions of Cass running and drinking and sinking into degradation, and also in the dream visions and memories that pervade the novel. Peter is troubled by dreams of treachery and betrayal even before he discovers Cass's cartoon in the Sunday *Times*. His dreams suggest that he never faced, or that he suppressed, the reality of his Italian experience, and also that he was an accomplice to some vague crime. His long dialogue with Cass is one of gradual discovery, but the nature of the crime is more than what is encompassed in Mason's raping of Francesca, Saverio's brutal murder, and Cass's misguided revenge on Mason. For the crime lies buried even in the mind of Cass, who mistakenly feels that he has come to terms with it, and it is expressed in his dreams and memories.

Cass's first important dream is a kind of extension of Peter's and suggests that Styron was developing his two characters as doubles. It begins in Raleigh, with his uncle driving him to the state prison, its high stone walls and guard towers foreshadowing the villa of Sambuco. Cass does not know the nature of his crime "other than that I had done something unspeakably wicked." When the steel gate clangs behind him he knows that his uncle has betrayed him or forgotten him, and his next thought, filling him with almost as much despair, is that the prison will be at least half full of Negroes. "I'd be spending the rest of my life among niggers" — this despite his belief that he had been long emancipated from such prejudice. Then the dream shifts and the real horror commences: "The prisoners had all gathered around me and were pointing at me, and sneering, and looking at me with hate and loathing and disgust, and calling me filthy names; and I heard one of them say: 'Any man that'd do that should be gassed!' Then I heard the others start to hoot and holler and shout: 'Gas him! Gas the dirty sonofabitch!' "

The next important dream, a Dostoevskian nightmare, comes after he has watched with helpless compassion an ageless peasant woman, "pop-eyed with toil, sweating, bent over like a broken limb beneath the everlasting load of fagots." She makes a "final desperate humping motion with her back but the enormous hummock of wood, badly balanced and off-kilter, came tumbling off her shoulders and fell to the cobblestones." In his dream he is riding in a bus along the mountain roads, and the bus driver, speeding through a village, runs over a dog. "All of its hinder parts right on up to its chest had been smashed flat — flat as those cutlets that the butcher down the street makes out of those thick slices of beef after pounding on them for half an hour." But the dog is still living, whimpering, its eyes rolling, trying to lift itself from the earth with its forepaws. The bus driver fetches a big stick and beats the dog on the head furiously, trying desperately to put the dog out of its misery. But the dog refuses to die and suffers miserably, "still trying to rise, while all the time the fellow kept thrashing away at his skull, hoping to free the beast from his torture." Then Cass sees that it is no longer the dog's head but that of the peasant woman with the fagots. "Lying there crushed and mangled, with her poor tormented body pressed against the dust, she let out piteous cries, shrieking, 'God! God! . . . Release me from this misery!' And each time she called out, *down* would come the flailing stick."

Accustomed to the associative connections of dreams, we are tempted to fit the elements of Cass's nightmares into a neat symbolic pattern. There is the vague, enormous crime, the betrayal by his family, the expressions of guilt, the alienation. There are the specific social evils: the treatment of blacks, prisoners being gassed, like Jews, the inexorable peasant poverty. Symbolic connections can no doubt be found by the careful reader, but such an exercise could obscure, indeed contradict, the primary fictional experience, which is one of disconnection. It would be more fitting to see Styron using the dreams to reinforce our feeling of unreasonable disconnectedness. It is not the links, then, but the gaps that are meaningful — between the clanging of the steel gate and the betrayal by his uncle, between his despair at being abandoned and his surge of prejudice, between his prejudice and his shame and his identification with gassed prisoners. Just as there is no linking reason for the peasant woman's unspeakable misery, and for torture to be the only form of humane charity. This disconnection is reinforced by the unreasonable resemblance of the peasant woman bearing her load of fagots to Saverio bearing his mountain of Peter's tourist baggage, and also between the accident with the speeding bus and Peter's accident with the motorscooter. Saverio and Luciano are the tragic and comic embodiments of wanton irresponsibility, the power which governs the world of the novel. And Cass is as wrong as the reader who sees the enormous crime in terms of social injustice. And wrong in thinking that he can redeem himself by bringing medicine to the dying peasant, or by reconciling himself to his family in the back country of South Carolina.

He is also wrong in placing his faith in art. This is shown in his unreasonable and sentimental reaction to his Paris vision. After forcing Poppy and the children to leave the apartment, he gazes out the window at the shabby street. The window is framed with huge elephant vines, swarming with ladybugs. He gazes at the web of a golden spider in the crotch of one of the vines. And he smells the baking of bread, listens to the music, and finds all his hatred and poison lost or forgotten. "I don't know quite how to describe it — this *bone-breaking* moment of loveliness. . . . It was as if I had been given for an instant the capacity to understand not just beauty itself by its outward signs, but the other — the *else*ness in beauty, this continuity of beauty in the scheme of all life which triumphs even to the point of taking in sordidness and shabbiness and ugliness." Many critics conclude that Cass is finding himself as an artist in the end, but it is important to remember that he is escaping from the modern world and from his complex responsibilities to it. Nor does Styron bring his own turbulent vision into an affirmative harmony.

Cass is wrong in thinking that he can turn his rejection of life into an affirmation. In the end he tells Peter that "as for being and nothingness, the one thing I did know was that to choose between them was simply to choose being, not for the sake of being, or even the love of being, much less the desire to be forever — but in the hope of being what I could be for a time." The world of this novel is finally no different from that of *Lie Down in Darkness* or *The Long March*. Peyton could not choose being because it was dominated by the agon between her mother and her father, because there was no center, because there was nothing to choose. Mannix could not choose being because being was served and expressed by Templeton. Cass cannot choose being because being is dominated by the power of wanton irresponsibility, and because it will yield no harmony or connection.

The experience of disconnection is also reinforced by two important memories in the novel. The first is unfocused. As in his earlier novels war is the condition of life, and World War II rumbles beneath the surface as a powerful undercurrent. Cass fought in the war and ended in the psychiatric ward. He recalls his conversations with the psychiatrist, and although, or perhaps because, there are no recollections of what led him to the psychiatric ward, these conversations seem to be the beginning of his search. Moreover, the novel is set in postwar Italy, Mason buys his supplies at the PX, and Cass's most meaningful conversations are with the fascist policeman, Luigi. America, as Cass's father suggested, has never suffered sufficiently to come to terms with reality, and Cass must confront reality in a war-torn land where totalitarianism and defeat were experienced and remain visible.

The second memory is focused. It is of Cass when he was a boy working in a Western Auto store deep in the back country of

Virginia — far removed in time and space from the present time in Sambuco. Cass and Lonnie, the redneck clerk, drove out to "dispossess" a radio from a Negro farmer who had failed to keep up with his payments. They entered the empty shack to search. "Lonnie, stubbing his toe against a sprung floorboard, finally reached down behind the planking and, triumphant, fished up the pathetic radio — white, plastic, already cracked, not much larger than a box of salt or rice, which had brought witchery in the night and tinny bright sounds of singing and laughter. 'Hid it!' said Lonnie. 'The *wise* sonofabitch.' " And spying the crack in the plastic, he cried, " 'We'll see about who breaks what!' And then pivoted on his toes, and with the other leg outthrust like a fullback punting a football shot a cowboy-boot-shod foot out against the flimsy kitchen table, hard, and brought the whole clutter of china cups and plates and saucers, sugar in cans, flour and meal and bacon fat, down to the floor in one monstrous and godawful detonation." And Cass remembers how a "tremendous warm excitement came over me, a feeling that — well, it was almost a feeling of anger, too, as if I'd picked up some of this young lout of a maniac's fury and was set on teaching the niggers, too. By God, this feeling, you know, I remember it — it was in my loins, hot, flowing, sexual. I knew it was wrong, I knew it, I knew it — bestial, horrible, abominable . . . but it was as if once I'd lost my courage anyway, once I'd given in — like some virgin, you see, who's finally stopped struggling and said to hell with it — then I could actually do what I was doing almost even with a sense of righteousness."

The whole incident is narrated with a finer sense of detail, character, and feeling than anything else in the novel. It is a memory which has been exercising strong unconscious pressures on Cass, for he has been dreaming of Negroes. But it is the most unconnected incident in the book. It could be said that Styron was not able to fully develop or imagine the wellsprings of Cass's character. But the novel has a powerful effect, and the effect results from the disconnections. Cass is haunted by expressions of violence that are not congruent with mental and physical surfaces. He insists to Peter that the genteel southerners and the northern liberals were ignorant or blind to the kind of experience into which Lonnie initiated him. And beneath the surface that Americans have created to disguise life also lie the violence of possessiveness, expressed in Mason's manipulation of Cass, the violence of arrogance, expressed by the movie company taking over Sambuco, the violence of class division, expressed in the life of the peasant woman with her mountain of fagots, the violence of laissez-faire individualism, expressed in the rape of Francesca, the violence of carelessness expressed by the bus driver running over the dog.

It is absolutely consistent with the nature of the novel for Cass's undirected striving to culminate in a sequence of actions out of a grade B movie — the rape, the murder, the chase to the cliff top — in a meretricious form that gives a false sense of excitement, resolution, and meaning. But the real culmination is the recognition that the murder of Francesca was an accident — Francesca happening to pass Saverio, responding hysterically not because of his innocent touch but because she had just been raped by Mason, and enflaming a lustful violence — and that Cass's revenge was a mistake. The real culmination, then, is an experience of accident, mistake, or random violence, which is totally incongruent with the logic of the melodramatic scene enacted by Mason, Francesca, and Cass. And the recognition should remind us of the incongruity between the disconnected violations in Cass's dreams, recollections, and his life as an expatriate, on the one hand, and on the other, his pattern of quest and redemption.

Opposed to and lying beneath the forms which offer a false sense of meaning and hope lies a violence that has a capricious life of its own, and which is expressed in violations that are absolutely unreasonable. This is the violation — of senseless surprise, absurd humiliation, and the recognition that it was all a mistake — which young Styron experienced as a marine recruit, and which he imaginatively transformed into the image of Mannix hanging high up in space with two drunks holding onto his slippery heels. This ultimate form of violence and violation derives from a power that has total control. In *The Long March* this power is served by Colonel Templeton. In *Set This House on Fire* it is manifested by allusions to totalitarianism in the references to World War II, the setting in Italy, the relation of Mason to Cass, the vengeance of Lonnie, the conversations with Luigi. That totalitarianism is only alluded to, that it escapes clear articulation, makes it all the more frightening. For the most terrifying form of total violation is when the power is unseen, unseeable, unknown, and unknowable. Frederick Hoffman, in *The Mortal No,* traces the history of violence from the period when assailant and victim could physically contend to the modern period, where the assailant is "impersonal, unreasonable, unreal, and unseen," where the assailant, in fact, has become the landscape. Kafka has made this experience most palpable in *The Trial*; therefore it is no wonder that Cass's dream of being imprisoned, abandoned, and threatened with gassing comes so close to the experience in Kafka's novel.

What makes the assailant or the power unseeable and unknowable is that it is literally formless and totally contradictory. Cass strives for the pure form of artistic harmony and of the God of love and salvation, but the power that energizes his world is an anti-form, like the Beast of Revelation. Most critics see Cass as having found salvation — love and harmony — in the reconciliation with his family, in the pastoral retreat, in the acceptance of his own limitations as an artist. But it seems to me that Styron

35

was working intellectually at odds with his imaginative discoveries. He shows Cass's house set on fire. And what he exposes in the images, energies, and conflicting patterns of the novel is the perpetual conflagration, the eternal apocalypse suppressed beneath the meretricious surface of American life and the false hopefulness of Christianity. Luciano will thrive in this world. New Saverios will emerge. And Cass, like Styron, will not fully accept the lessons of hell, or learn from Luigi, the Italian who has stoically accommodated to modern reality. Cass, like Styron, intellectually simplifies the apocalyptic conflict and sees it in terms of melodrama, retaining his American optimism, and retreating to a primal Eden, which is as unrealistic and inconsistent with the novel's experience as Cass's vision from the Paris window.

In *The Confessions of Nat Turner* (1967) Styron worked out the pattern of redemption more fully, and the simplification leads to new social and aesthetic problems. Both Cass and Nat are redeemed by kinds of divine intercession, or *deus ex machina*. Cass is apparently redeemed by the miraculous appearance and the gratuitous murder of Francesca. First she leads him to change his life and selflessly serve her dying father, then she leads him to become her avenging hero, and finally she leads him away from the Old World where reality is inescapable, and back to the New World where, from the very beginning, reality has been suppressed by restorations of the Garden of Eden.

Nat Turner is inspired by two gods. A Negro slave educated by a benevolent white master and enjoying the relative ease of a house servant, he is turned into a fanatic by the God of Ezekiel, who comes to him in a vision, and inspires him to lead a vengeful and slaughterous revolt against the slavemasters of Southampton County, Virginia. And he is redeemed by the voice of the murdered Margaret Whitehead, coming to him in his prison cell and speaking to him in words of love from the New Testament. Both the Old Testament God of vengeance and the New Testament God of love turn Nat Turner away from the social reality of slavery in the American South. As in *Set This House on Fire*, the *deus ex machina* serves as an ethical, psychological, and artistic evasion.

Not that Styron was looking for an easy way out. Quite the contrary. What makes Styron's development as a writer so exhilarating to follow is just the difficulty and the magnitude of the challenges he seeks out, somewhat in the manner of Captain Mannix and Cass Kinsolving. In an interview with Robert Canzoneri and Page Stegner he claims that "one of the central mystiques of the writer of novels is that . . . you take the hardest way in order to see if you can surmount the problems. And I know that imposing upon myself this kind of tension has, to my mind, produced whatever good stuff I've ever produced." The challenge which Styron set for himself in this novel was one that no white southern writer had ever accepted, to "enter into the consciousness of a Negro in the early decades of the 19th century," in fact to become the unique individual of Nat Turner by narrating the story of his rebellion from his point of view.

Very little is known about Nat Turner. The closest thing to firsthand evidence is a twenty-page confession dictated to Thomas Gray, the white lawyer who served both the defense and the prosecution and who edited what he heard for the white jury and the white press. This compounded the challenge to Styron and led ten black writers to publish a critical attack on this volume, initiating a debate of great sociological and political importance. Styron's Nat Turner, then, is the product of a creative imagination, which the white southern historian C. Vann Woodward claims is "informed by a respect for history, a sure feeling for the period, and a deep and precise sense of place and time," but which most black writers claim is racist in its selection of data and distortion of black psychology.

In order to enter Nat's consciousness most fully, Styron chose the point in time after the abortive rebellion, after Nat committed his one act of violence and murdered Margaret Whitehead, just when, as Styron imagines it, Turner felt bereft of God. "The relationship with God seemed to be the central thing in my own conception of the man. The book ends on the day of his execution, and part of it is the story of his redemption." Part of Nat Turner's story may have been of redemption, although in the original confessions, Turner seemed to deny the need for redemption when he responded to Gray: "*Ques.* Do you not find yourself mistaken now? *Ans.* Was not Christ crucified?" But Styron made this part dominant when he shaped the story of Nat Turner's life into the pattern of fall and return to grace. And, more important, the redemptive pattern conflicts with and obscures the patterns of social and psychological insights.

Katherine Ellis, in an essay which analyzed the "true confession story," illuminates a pattern that can be found in *The Confessions of Nat Turner*. The "true confession" heroine whether she leaves her suburban home to become a streetwalker, or dances naked at her high school prom, is dissatisfied with her life, renounces the security and propriety of the middle class, and follows a path of self-destructive excess. Salvation appears unexpectedly and is usually unmotivated — the husband goes through a change of character, the boyfriend, who did not really renounce her but was detained by some irrelevant circumstance, returns — and the heroine suddenly sees the light. What she sees is that *she* has been wrong. The "true confession" always locates the fault within the heroine and never within the society that produced the conditions for her fall. And the reader finishes the story with a vicarious purgation and the happy feeling that in America everything turns out for the best.

In Styron's first two works there is no *deus ex machina* and no redemption. In *Set This House on Fire* there is enough in the novel to counteract the pattern of redemption; the pattern can be seen as part of the larger conflicting structure. Moreover Cass's rebellion is, in Ihab Hassan's terms, a "metaphysical rebellion" in the tradition of Ivan Karamazov and Captain Ahab, which is against the perpetual injustice of God's world. But in *The Confessions of Nat Turner,* while the rebellion is social, the redemptive pattern is dominant. And the movement toward redemption undermines the basis for rebellion. The outspoken criticism in *Ten Black Writers Respond* may be misguided in taking Styron to task for distorting history; a writer is under no obligation to be true to the facts, especially when the facts are so few and uncertain. But they are right in seeing Styron's Nat Turner as being oblivious to the social reality which he claims to respond to. And they are also right in seeing that Styron shows the flaw to be not within the system of slavery but within the mind of the rebel.

In an interview for the *New York Times* Styron describes the major conflict as one between the values and morality of the Old and the New Testament: "savagery and revenge" versus "charity and brotherhood." And the novel ends with Nat's realization that Margaret Whitehead, or perhaps his murdering this gentle white girl, " '*showed me Him whose presence I had not fathomed or maybe never even known.'* " So while Styron describes the system of slavery which not only violated the black man but completely traumatized him, "dehumanized the slave and divested him of his honor, moral responsibility, and manhood," he shifts his attention to what he describes as the "fateful impulse" which "brought Nat to disaster." The novel is ultimately confused because Styron shifts the disaster and the blame from without to within; the fault lies not in the social structure but within Nat's mind. It is this judgment that the black critics define as racist.

The issue of racism has been fully explored by the ten black writers and in Styron's replies. What I am pointing to here is a weakness in the novel that derives from Styron's ambivalence, which kept him from fully realizing either the social or the psychological possibilities. As Richard Gilman shows, the "whole physical construction, this thick detail, this 'sensitivity' to nature and lyric evocation of place, is all irrelevant to Nat Turner as a fictional creation, has nothing to do with his conflicts or hopes or fears, with his position within the field of fictional energies . . . with the moral or existential meanings which presumably Styron is pursuing." One of Styron's outstanding strengths as a novelist is in his descriptions, his evocations of place, which worked so well either to reinforce or to counterpoint the dramatic scenes in his earlier works, but in this novel they betray his uncertainty. Another of his strengths is in his handling of action, but here it leads to a simplification of his psychological insights.

Margaret Whitehead served Styron as a psychological springboard. The story of Nat Turner had been working in his mind since he read the original confessions in the late forties, and he had planned to make Turner the subject of his second novel. Years later, having finally started to write *The Confessions*, he traveled back to the scene of the rebellion, and as he approached the house of Mrs. Catherine Whitehead, he "tried to recollect its particular role in Nat's destiny." Then he remembered:

There was something baffling, secret, irrational about Nat's own participation in the uprising. He was unable to kill. Time and time again in his confession one discovers him saying (in an offhand tone; one must dig for the implications): "I could not give the death blow, the hatchet glanced from his head," or, "I struck her several blows over the head, but I was unable to kill her as the sword was dull . . ." It is too much to believe, over and over again: the glancing hatchet, the dull sword. It smacks rather, as in *Hamlet*, of rationalization, ghastly fear, an access of guilt, a shrinking from violence, and fatal irresolution. Alone here at this house, turned now into a huge corncrib around which pigs rooted and snorted in the silence of a spring afternoon, here alone was Nat finally able — or was he forced? — to commit a murder, and this upon a girl of eighteen named Margaret Whitehead, described by Drewry . . . as "the belle of the county." The scene is apocalyptic — afternoon bedlam in the wild harsh sunlight and August heat.

Styron shows Nat Turner to be motivated by the sublimation of his desire for the white woman of his dreams, who finally takes the form of Margaret Whitehead. In the interview with Canzoneri and Stegner, Styron points to the complexity of such sublimation when he explains the "love-hate relationship" between Nat, the puritanic but virile young man, and the "unconsciously flirtatious" eighteen-year-old white girl "who's the only nubile girl, so far as I can find out, killed during the insurrection": "The barrier is incredible, but it's tissue paper thin, and for just that reason it's all the more impermeable. And so the way that you break it down is in the most apocalyptic way that is possible to a human being. You break through it by killing." Louis Rubin makes an even better case for Styron when he inteprets Nat Turner's real rebellion to derive not so much from his bondage or his exploitation but from society's depriving him of his right to love and be loved. "The world he inhabits is such that at best he can expect from whites only pity, and at worst outright hatred, while from his fellow slaves he can expect only inarticulate admiration at best, and at worst envy and contempt. Thus he cannot *give* himself to anyone. No one wants him for what he is. For everyone, white and black, friend and foe, he must play a role. . . . Denied, therefore, the right to give himself, to love, Nat can only hate, and the result is destruction."

Both Styron's observation and Rubin's interpretation tell us

41

much about the potential of Nat's characterization, but unfortunately the novel is not developed to realize these complex insights or to make us feel their emotional impact. Margaret Whitehead is a paper character, cut from the pattern of southern romance. And her relation with Nat is too transparent a device, designed to reveal impulses which Styron in his interview for the *New York Times* defines as, "historically speaking, those of the traditional revolutionary — that is to say puritanical, repressive and sublimated." Nat Turner is a weak character not because of Styron's "racism," nor because it is impossible for a white man to create a successful black revolutionary. It is because Turner, billed as a unique and complex character, is diminished or explained away by such simplified psychology. This is not to say that Styron was wrong in seeing the traditional revolutionary as puritanical, repressive, and sublimated, just that he did not go far enough in developing this potential. We need only look for an example to Peter Weiss's characterization of Marat, whose sublimations are convincing and interesting, and who still emerges as heroic — and as a revolutionary.

The challenge that exercised Styron's imagination was to enter the consciousness of Nat Turner, to tell the story from his point of view. We are led to wonder whether Styron might have developed Nat Turner more convincingly and more interestingly, whether he might indeed have grappled more strenuously with the enigma of Nat's character, by choosing a different vantage — by learning from his experience in *The Long March* and *Set This House on Fire* to gain some distance on a man of heroic proportions. A secondary character — black or white, historical or contemporary, trying to comprehend the meager facts of the original confession necessarily distorted by the lawyer who transcribed it for the white jury — might develop the ironies and the clashes of perspective, might deepen and expand the scope of the novel, might leave Nat Turner an engaging enigma.

The failure of *The Confessions* may well be due to Styron's integrity and daring. For if in his early works he was bridging the experiences of the twenties and fifties, here he is building a bridge to a generation not content to view life as an accident, to see man as a clown suffering violation and indignity, or to accept injustice as irremediable. It may be that this view caused him to fall back on a pattern that obscures the realities of Nat Turner's world and of our own. But what makes Styron's development so exhilarating to follow is that like Mannix and Cass he takes "the hardest way," seeks out the existential challenge, and embodies the conflict between Christian humanism and a world that denies such values. He believes in the traditional novel form, with its faith in character, plot, and ultimate knowledge. Yet at his best he evokes a world where irrational warfare is the condition of life, a world that undermines psychological connections, temporal causation, and any kind of certainty. If Styron is ambivalent, he makes us suffer the ambivalence — suffer the loss of humane values while remaining engaged in a struggle to preserve them.

⨯ Selected Bibliography

Works of William Styron

BOOKS

Lie Down in Darkness. New York: Bobbs-Merrill, 1951.
The Long March. New York: Random House, 1956.
Set This House on Fire. New York: Random House, 1960.
The Confessions of Nat Turner. New York: Random House, 1967.

SHORT STORIES

"Autumn," *One and Twenty: Duke Narrative and Verse, 1924–1945,* edited by
W. Blackburn. Durham, N.C.: Duke University Press, 1945.
"The Long Dark Road," *One and Twenty: Duke Narrative and Verse, 1924–
1945,* edited by W. Blackburn. Durham, N.C.: Duke University Press, 1945.
"A Moment in Trieste," *American Vanguard, 1948,* edited by Don M. Wolfe.
Ithaca, N.Y.: Cornell University Press, 1948.
"The Enormous Window," *American Vanguard, 1950,* edited by Charles I.
Glicksberg. New York: New School for Social Research, 1950.
"[The] Long March," *discovery No. 1,* edited by John W. Aldridge and Vance
Bourjaily. New York: Pocket Books, 1953.
"The McCabes," *Paris Review,* 6:12–28 (Autumn–Winter 1960). (Part of Chapter VI of *Set This House on Fire.*)

ARTICLES AND REVIEWS

"Letter to an Editor," *Paris Review,* 1:9–13 (Spring 1953).
"The Prevalence of Wonders," *Nation,* 176:370–71 (May 2, 1953).
"The Paris Review," *Harper's Bazaar,* 87:122, 173 (August 1953).
"What's Wrong with the American Novel?" *American Scholar,* 24:464–503
(Autumn 1955).
"If You Write for Television . . ." *New Republic,* 140:16 (April 6, 1959). (On
the television adaptation of *The Long March.*)
"Introduction," *Best Short Stories from the Paris Review.* New York: Dutton,
1959.
"Mrs. Aadland's Little Girl, Beverly," *Esquire,* 56:142, 189–91 (November 1961).

44

"The Death-in-Life of Benjamin Reid," *Esquire*, 57:114, 141–45 (February 1962).

"As He Lay Dead, a Bitter Grief," *Life*, 53:39–42 (July 20, 1962). (On Faulkner's funeral.)

"The Aftermath of Benjamin Reid," *Esquire*, 58:79, 81, 158, 160, 164 (November 1962).

"Two Writers Talk It Over," *Esquire*, 60:57–59 (July 1963). (Styron and James Jones.)

"Overcome," *New York Review of Books*, 1:18–19 (September 26, 1963). (Review of Herbert Aptheker's *American Slave Revolts*.)

"An Elegy for F. Scott Fitzgerald," *New York Review of Books*, 1:1–3 (November 28, 1963).

"The Habit," *New York Review of Books*, 1:13–14 (December 26, 1963).

"A Southern Conscience," *New York Review of Books*, 2:3 (April 2, 1964).

"Tootsie Rolls," *New York Review of Books*, 2:8 (May 14, 1964).

"MacArthur's Reminiscences," *New York Review of Books*, 3:3–5 (October 8, 1964).

"This Quiet Dust," *Harper's*, 230:134–46 (April 1965).

"Vice That Has No Name," *Harper's*, 236:97–100 (February 1966).

"William Styron Replies," *Nation*, 544–47 (April 22, 1968). (Reply to Herbert Aptheker's review of *Nat Turner*.)

"The Shade of Thomas Wolfe," *Harper's*, 236:96–104 (April 1968).

"Oldest America," *McCall's*, 95:94, 123 (July 1968).

"My Generation," *Esquire*, 70:123–24 (October 1968).

CURRENT AMERICAN REPRINTS

The Confessions of Nat Turner. New York: New American Library. $1.25.

Lie Down in Darkness. New York: Compass Books. $1.65. New York: Modern Library. $2.45. New York: New American Library. $.95.

The Long March. New York: New American Library. $.75. New York: Vintage Books. $1.25.

Set This House on Fire. New York: New American Library. $.95.

Critical and Biographical Studies

Baumbach, Jonathan. *The Landscape of Nightmare*. New York: New York University Press, 1965.

Brandriff, Welles T. "The Rule of Order and Disorder in *The Long March*," *English Journal*, 56:54–59 (January 1967).

Canzoneri, Robert, and Page Stegner. "An Interview with William Styron," *Per/Se*, 1:37–44 (Summer 1966).

Clarke, John H., editor. *William Styron's Nat Turner: Ten Black Writers Respond*. Boston: Beacon, 1968. (Includes Turner's *Confessions*.)

Davis, Robert Gorham. "The American Individualist Tradition: Bellow and Styron," *The Creative Present*, edited by Norma Balakian and Charles Simmons. New York: Doubleday, 1963.

———. "Styron and the Students," *Critique*, 3:37–46 (Summer 1960).

Dempsey, David. "Talk with William Styron," *New York Times Book Review*, September 9, 1951, p. 27.

Fossum, Robert H. *William Styron: A Critical Essay*. Grand Rapids, Mich.: William B. Eerdmans, 1968.

Friedman, Melvin J. "William Styron: An Interim Appraisal," *English Journal*, 50:149–58, 192 (March 1961).

Galloway, David D. *The Absurd Hero in American Fiction*. Austin, Texas: University of Texas Press, 1966.

Geismar, Maxwell. *American Moderns*. New York: Hill and Wang, 1958.

Gilman, Richard. "Nat Turner Revisited," *New Republic*, 158:23–32 (April 27, 1968).

Gossett, Louise Y. *Violence in Recent Southern Fiction*. Durham, N.C.: Duke University Press, 1965.

Hassan, Ihab. "The Novel of Outrage: A Minority Voice in Postwar American Fiction," *American Scholar*, 34:239–53 (Spring 1965).

———. *Radical Innocence*. Princeton, N.J.: Princeton University Press, 1961.

Hoffman, Frederick J. "The Cure of 'Nothing!': The Fiction of William Styron," *Frontiers of American Culture*, edited by Ray B. Browne *et al.* Indianapolis, Ind.: Purdue University Press, 1968.

Kauffmann, Stanley. "Styron's Unwritten Novel," *Hudson Review*, 20:675–80 (Winter 1967–68).

Klotz, Marvin. "The Triumph over Time: Narrative Form in William Faulkner and William Styron," *Mississippi Quarterly*, 17:9–20 (Winter 1963–64).

Matthiessen, Peter, and George Plimpton. "The Art of Fiction," *Paris Review*, 2:42–57 (Spring 1954). Reprinted in *Writers at Work: The Paris Review Interviews*, edited by Malcolm Cowley. New York: Viking, 1958.

Monaghan, Charles. "Portrait of a Man Reading," *Book World*, 2:8 (October 27, 1968). (Interview with Styron.)

Nigro, August. "*The Long March*: The Expansive Hero in a Closed World," *Critique*, 9:103–12 (No. 3, 1967).

O'Connell, Shaun. "The Expense of Spirit: The Vision of William Styron," *Critique*, 8:20–33 (Winter 1966).

Plimpton, George. "William Styron: A Shared Ordeal," *New York Times Book Review*, October 8, 1967, pp. 2, 3, 30, 32, 34. (Interview with Styron.)

Roth, Philip. "Writing American Fiction," *Commentary*, 31:222–33 (March 1961).

Rubin, Louis D., Jr. *The Faraway Country*. Seattle: University of Washington Press, 1963.

———. "Notes on the Literary Scene: Their Own Language," *Harper's*, 230:173–75 (April 1965).

———. "The South and the Faraway Country," *Virginia Quarterly Review*, 38:444–59 (Summer 1962).

———. "William Styron and Human Bondage: *The Confessions of Nat Turner*," *Hollins Critic*, 4:1–12 (December 1967).

Sokolov, Raymond. "Into the Mind of Nat Turner," *Newsweek*, 70:65–69 (October 16, 1967).

Stevenson, David L. "Styron and the Fiction of the Fifties," *Critique*, 3:47–58 (Summer 1960).

Thelwell, Mike. "Back with the Wind: Mr. Styron and the Reverend Turner," in *William Styron's Nat Turner: Ten Black Writers Respond*, edited by John H. Clarke. Boston: Beacon Press, 1968.

Urang, Gunnar. "The Broader Vision: William Styron's *Set This House on Fire*," *Critique*, 8:47–69 (Winter 1966).

Waldmeir, Joseph. "Quest without Faith," *Nation*, 193:390–96 (November 18, 1961).

Winner, Arthur. "Adjustment, Tragic Humanism and Italy," *Studi Americani*, 7:311–61 (1961).

9268   190